Totally New

Totally New

Diane Blacker

Fleming H. Revell Company
Old Tappan, New Jersey

All Scripture quotations in this volume unless otherwise identified are from The Living Bible, Copyright © 1971 by Tyndale House Publishers, Wheaton, Illinois 60187. All rights reserved.

Scripture quotation identified KJV is from The King James Version of the Bible.

Diane Blacker is a Total Woman instructor. The material in this book is not a part of the Total Woman course.

Mrs. Blacker may be reached at P.O. Box 325, Lake Bluff, Illinois 60044.

Library of Congress Cataloging in Publication Data

Blacker, Diane.
    Totally new.

    Includes bibliographical references.
    1. Christian life—1960-   I. Title.
BV4501.2.B54   248'.4   76-10249
ISBN 0-8007-0787-7

This letter is written to each of you, who have so recently placed your faith in Jesus Christ as your Savior and Lord. May you experience the inexpressible joy of a life that is Totally New.

Acknowledgments

My appreciation is expressed to:

Dr. Robert Strong, for ten years my pastor-teacher and friend. He is presently serving as Professor of Homiletics, Reformed Theological Seminary, Jackson, Mississippi. Words are not adequate to express the gratitude I feel in my heart for his faithful preaching of God's Word.

Dr. Gilbert Peterson, Chairman of the Christian Education Department, Trinity Evangelical Divinity School, Deerfield, Illinois, for his guidance and suggestions which have been incorporated into the final print.

Contents

Foreword

Diane Blacker exemplifies all that is totally wonderful about a Total Woman. I'm so proud that she is a Total Woman instructor.

- She is a loving wife and mother.
- She is a warm, friendly, concerned, and sympathetic person.
- She is a dear sister in Christ and a true friend.

For God so loved the world, that he gave his only begotten Son, that whosoever believeth in him should not perish, but have everlasting life.

Diane, who teaches Total Woman classes across the United States, is one of our finest and most energetic instructors. She has always had a special burden for new Christians—many had never before read the Bible or gone to church prior to attending Total Woman classes. To help establish them in their new-found faith, she has written this guidebook which Diane calls *Totally New*.

As I wrote in *The Total Woman*, "Don't keep the faith . . . pass it on." This is what Diane Blacker has done through this written ministry. May all who read it find the peace and love of Christ, and discover the ageless truth:

John 3:16 KJV

Marabel Morgan

1

Totally New . . .
A Letter to New Christians

Welcome to God's family—where wondrous events are happening every day—just like the one that happened in your life, when the Lord Jesus touched you and made you *Totally New*. Yes, that's what God promised when you opened your heart and life to Jesus. In that moment, you became a brand-new person inside.

What could be more exciting than a fresh start in life? Every day can be special in some new way. May this letter help you to get to know the One Person in all the world who loves you the most—Jesus Christ, our Lord.

The Bible is God's Word given to those who have placed their faith and trust in His Son, Jesus. Tucked away in each chapter are promises that He has made to us. As you begin to read the books that are in the Bible, you will discover how God has made a provision for each of life's needs. I wish I could share all of them with you, but for now we will have to settle for just a few.

In the pages of this letter, we are going to look at passages of Scripture written through the inspiration of God's Holy Spirit, by two of Jesus' Apostles, John and Paul. Their books have done so much to help new Christians to a full understanding of what it means to be a Christian.

There will also be verses from the Book of Psalms. As you begin your new life with Jesus, my prayer for you is found in the Book of Ephesians, chapter 3, verses 17-19, where Paul writes, "And I pray that Christ will be more and more at home in your hearts, living within you as you trust in him. May your roots go down deep into the soil of God's marvelous love; and may you be able to feel and understand, as all God's children should, how long, how wide, how deep, and how high his love really is; and to experience this love for yourselves, though it is so great that you will never see the end of it or fully know or understand it. And so at last you will be filled up with God himself."

In the brief moment of prayer, when you opened your heart to Jesus, many things happened in your life. You were born into God's family, His Holy Spirit came into your life to dwell within your heart and soul, your sins were forgiven, and this totally new life began. You may be aware of some things already, but perhaps there are a few question marks, too!

That is the way it should be. You cannot be expected to know everything about Jesus when you first meet Him, any more than you would be expected to know those new neighbors who just moved in down the street. As you spend time with new friends, the friendship grows and often a real bond of love and devotion to the other person develops. This is the way it will be with Jesus. As you spend time with Him and get to know Him, His love will overwhelm you. When you know that you are loved *that* way, it is only natural that you respond in love to Him.

For now you probably want to know what took place that wonderful moment and what will happen in the days and months to come. Each person is unique. There is not a carbon copy of you anywhere. In the same respect, no two people ever come to Jesus in exactly the same way. Some of you simply responded in quiet assurance that this was the void—the missing ingredient in your life. For some there were tears of relief or joy. Others came in the midst of great inner turmoil or heartache.

Regardless of your experience, for each of you the important thing is that now you are here. The Bible calls coming to Jesus your "conversion." This means that the pattern of your life takes on a new purpose and direction under the guidance of the Holy Spirit of God. The Apostle Paul explains this in his letter in 2 Corinthians 5:17, 18, "When someone becomes a Christian he becomes a brand new person inside. He is not the same any more. A new life has begun! All these new things are from God who brought us back to himself through what Christ Jesus did. . . ."

2

Who Is Jesus and What Did He Do?

Jesus is God and Jesus is Man. He is the only God-Man. He is the Creator of all things in heaven and earth and He is also our Savior. Paul's letter to the Colossians says in chapter 1 verses 15-19: "Christ is the exact likeness of the unseen God. He existed before God made anything at all, and, in fact, Christ himself is the Creator who made everything in heaven and earth, the things we can see and the things we can't; the spirit world with its kings and kingdoms, its rulers and authorities; all were made by Christ for his own use and glory. He was before all else began and it is his power that holds everything together. He is the Head of the body made up of his people—that is, his church—which he began; and he is the Leader of all those who arise from the dead, so that he is first in everything; for God wanted all of himself to be in his Son.''

This passage of Scripture beautifully describes how Jesus is more than mere man and more than an extraordinary man. It shows us that indeed He is God, who took upon Himself the form of a man to do for us what we were incapable of doing for ourselves. He has always existed in His divine nature, yet humbled Himself to be born as a human being nearly 2,000 years ago.

Great prophets told of His coming, of His life, His death, and His Resurrection from the dead, hundreds of years before it happened. The Old Testament has over 300 references to Jesus, the Messiah. The life that Jesus led, the miracles He performed, the words He spoke, His death on the cross, His Resurrection from the dead, and His ascent into heaven verify the fact that He is who He claimed to be—the Messiah, the Savior of the world. In John 14:6 Jesus said, ''I am the Way—yes, and the Truth and the Life. No one can get to the Father except by means of me.'' John 14:11, ''. . . I am in the Father and the Father is in me.'' John 14:9, ''. . . . Anyone who has seen me has seen the Father!''

The forgiveness of sins is what Christ did for us when He willingly gave His life and shed His blood for us on the cross at Calvary. There is no other way our sins can be forgiven. He paid the price for our sin and ransomed us that morning when He was nailed to the tree, outside the Jerusalem walls. That's what we call the Gospel—the Good News! There is forgiveness of sins for all who accept Jesus as their Savior and Lord.

Paul tells about this great event so clearly in Colossians 1:20-23, "It was through what his Son did that God cleared a path for everything to come to him—all things in heaven and on earth—for Christ's death on the cross has made peace with God for all by his blood. This includes you who were once so far away from God. You were his enemies and hated him and were separated from him by your evil thoughts and actions, yet now he had brought you back as his friends. He has done this through the death on the cross of his own human body, and now as a result Christ has brought you into the very presence of God, and you are standing there before him with nothing left against you—nothing left that he could even chide you for; the only condition is that you fully believe the Truth, standing in it steadfast and firm, strong in the Lord, convinced of the Good News that Jesus died for you, and never shifting from trusting him to save you. This is the wonderful news that came to each of you and is now spreading all over the world. And I, Paul, have the joy of telling it to others."

Even though all of our sins are forgiven because of Jesus' shed blood on the cross, it is necessary for the Christian to confess the sins that took place in the past and the ones that occur each day. In this way, we appropriate what Jesus did. In the little letter John wrote near the end of the Bible, called 1 John 1:9, it says, "But if we confess our sins to him, he can be depended on to forgive us and to cleanse us from every wrong. . . ."

Confession means agreeing with God concerning the specific sins that are in our lives. God will show you the areas of your life that need to be confessed. Take a brief period of time by yourself today and ask God to reveal those things in your life that will hinder you from having the right kind of fellowship with Him. He won't be too hard on you! He will just show you a few things at first. As you grow, other areas will be revealed to you as you are able to deal with them. For now, even taking a piece of paper and writing down the things that God brings into your mind will help you to see your sin.

After you have spent some time in prayer and can no longer think of anything to write, claim that wonderful promise that you read from 1 John 1:9. Now you can rip that paper into pieces because those sins have been confessed and they are forgiven and you do not have to concern yourself with them again.

Sometimes we have done certain things that need to be made right with other people. There will be times when we will need to say we are sorry to someone whom we have wronged so our consciences can be cleared of any wrongdoing on our part. It is wonderful to know that now anytime sin enters our life, we can confess it immediately, be forgiven, and continue walking in unhindered fellowship with our Lord. We do not have to carry the burden of guilt or wrong actions over long periods of time. God is with us every moment. Talk to Him in quiet thoughts throughout the day. You don't have to wait for a certain time of the day or night, because He is always there.

3

Do Christians Sin?

When God gives us our new life, we have the old self with us, too. We have habits and thought patterns that can be hard to break, especially if the other members of our family and our friends are not Christians. Other people have a great influence on us and exert a lot of pressure in our lives. Some habits disappear quickly while others are very subtle and we may not even recognize them as being sin. Many of these subtle sins are actually the way we handle our responses to other people or our circumstances in life.

The Apostle Paul gives us quite a list of things in chapter 4, verses 17-32 of Ephesians. Included here are attitudes as well as actions. He names lying, anger, holding a grudge, dishonesty, bad language, meanness, revenge, quarreling, and harsh words. Other Bible passages refer to worry, anxiety, rebellion, hatred, resentment, bitterness, gossip, hostility, unkindness, and many other irritants that will, if we let them, fester within us, until they grow so far out of proportion that many areas of our lives will reflect these attitudes instead of Christ's attitudes. These things that were named are sins and must be confessed as sins. They are tricky and difficult for us to handle, but, praise God, they are not too difficult for Him. Read Romans 7:21-25.

God is always with you and will guide you every step of the way. His love is constant and His desire for the very best for your life never wavers. We are the ones who falter and get out of step. The Book of Hebrews 13:8 tells us that Jesus never changes, "Jesus Christ is the same yesterday, today, and forever."

The closer you stay to Jesus the more your life will begin to reflect the qualities that He gives. These qualities are spoken of in Galatians 5:22-25, "But when the Holy Spirit controls our lives he will produce this kind of fruit in us: love, joy, peace, patience, kindness, goodness, faithfulness, gentleness and self-control; and here there is no conflict with Jewish laws. Those who belong to Christ have nailed their evil desires to his cross and crucified them there. If we are living now by the Holy Spirit's power, let us follow the Holy Spirit's leading in every part of our lives."

The awareness of Christ's presence and power in your life through the indwelling of the Holy Spirit gives the Christian a freedom that no natural person will ever know. When we are not burdened with wrong attitudes and desires, we have for the first time in our lives the ability to grow and mature to our full potential. No chains to bind us, only the love of our Savior to give full meaning to each day of our lives. Galatians 5:13, 14. ". . . you have been given freedom . . . to love and serve each other. For the whole Law can be summed up in this one command: 'Love others as you love yourself.' "

Keep from the sins I mentioned by giving the control of your life over to God's Holy Spirit. Allow Him to direct your days, your actions, and your reactions. First Corinthians 10:13. "But remember this—the wrong desires that come into your life aren't anything new and different. Many others have faced exactly the same problems before you. *And* no temptation is irresistible. You can trust God to keep the temptation from becoming so strong that you can't stand up against it, for he has promised this and will do what he says. He will show you how to escape temptation's power so that you can bear up patiently against it."

4

Prayer–Talking With God

I used to have difficulty praying because I was never sure if my *Thee*s and *Thou*s were in the right places. As I began to read my Bible, I became aware that God already knew everything about me, physically, mentally, and spiritually. I had no secrets from Him (and He still loved me). What freedom—when I began just to talk to Him—everywhere I went, no matter what I was doing, He had time to listen. I could tell Him my joys and my sorrows, my fears and disappointments, my gratitude for His tender care, the thankfulness I felt when I knew He heard and was answering my prayers. At first, I even apologized because I was sure I had not prayed the way I should. I wanted Him to know that despite everything, my heart's desire was to be pleasing to Him.

Our prayers will vary as much as our needs. Many will be short "talks" or "sky telegrams" when we are in a tight spot. There will also be hours when we will agonize in prayer, when our needs seem desperate and we are near despair. In those moments remember the promise of Hebrews 13:5, 6, ". . . 'I will never, never fail you nor forsake you.' That is why we can say without any doubt or fear, 'The Lord is my Helper and I am not afraid of anything that mere man can do to me.' "

The times of prayer that I have mentioned above are part of your daily fellowship with Jesus. You will also want to establish a regular time of prayer each day as well. Most Christians include their time of prayer with the time they spend reading their Bibles. This is called our "quiet time." Your quiet time will be the most meaningful part of the day. It should be a time alone if possible where you will not have a lot of interruptions. When you are alone, you can really open your heart to God. There are certain elements that need to be present in our prayers at this time in order for us to receive the full blessing that God will give when we come to Him in prayer. I learned it in a way that is easy to remember: ACTS—*Adoration, Confession, Thanksgiving,* and *Supplication.*

Adoration: When we remember God's infinite greatness and His love for us, we cannot help but praise Him and worship Him with all of our being. When we think of His power—how He created a whole universe from nothing and yet He is so tender that He cares about everything in our lives—how can we help but adore Him and stand in awe of Him, with all reverence? We recognize that we are in His presence by the gift of His grace alone because of what Jesus did for us on the cross. If Jesus had not shed His blood in payment for our sins, we would not have access to God at all.

Confession: We talked about sin and how we must be forgiven. There is a verse in the Old Testament (Psalms 66:18) that deals with prayer. It says, "He [God] would not have listened if I had not confessed my sins." It is necessary to be cleansed from all known sins in your life. Remember 1 John 1:9? Nothing in our lives or our thoughts is hidden from God and so we must be completely honest, naming the specific sins—not just general areas.

Along with confession comes repentance. To repent of one's sins is to be sorry and ashamed of the wrongdoing, to have a change of heart and a sincere desire not to commit that act again. The Holy Spirit will convict you of the things in your life that need to be confessed and repented. Don't be concerned with things that may have taken place that you have forgotten. Concern of this kind leads to introspection and nothing is ever gained by dwelling on the past.

Concentrate on Jesus' love and forgiveness and the changes that need to be made in your life and behavior. We need to have a forgiving spirit toward others who have wronged us and forgive them in the same way God has forgiven us. Obedience to God's Word and a life that reflects the joy of knowing Jesus is the mark of a true Christian.

Thanksgiving: The truest demonstration of faith comes when we express our gratitude and thanks to God. Not only for our salvation, for our daily needs and answers to prayer, but also thank Him in advance for what He is going to do in our lives and in the lives of our loved ones. First Thessalonians 5:18 tells us, "No matter what happens, always be thankful, for this is God's will for you who belong to Christ Jesus." That is quite a verse and it means just what it says—to be thankful for everything, the good things, the sad things—trust Him for everything. This is not a blind faith, but a complete trust in Almighty God; the confidence and assurance that your life is guided and controlled by Him.

Supplication: This is humble, earnest prayer where we petition God for the needs and burdens of our lives. We ask for guidance and wisdom in dealing with our problems. We pray for strength of body and soul, and for the refreshing and filling of the Holy Spirit to empower our lives. Everything that concerns us concerns our Heavenly Father.

This is the time that we will want to pray for others also. Praying for others is called intercessory prayer. We intercede on behalf of our family members, friends, our nation, other Christians, and their work in making Jesus known. Many Christians keep a written prayer list or notebook, where they make a list of people for whom to pray and also other specific requests that they make to God. It is nice for you to have a place for the date that you begin to pray about each one and a place to record when the prayer is answered. If your prayer list is long, it can be divided into a weekly prayer calendar so that you pray for individual people or things on certain days of the week.

Our prayers are answered by God, though not always on our timetable. I have had many immediate answers, as when I pray for strength, guidance, courage, patience, and so forth. I have waited months and even years when praying for a loved one's salvation. God has said, "Keep praying and wait," and there are also times when His answer is, "No. That is not My desire for you."

When you are cleansed from all known sin, living to the best of your knowledge and ability in obedience to God's Word, praying with a believing heart, you can expect to receive answers to your prayers. (*See* John 16:24, 1 John 5:14, and Romans 8:26-28.)

5

What Is Faith, Trust, and Belief?

These three words are used interchangeably in the Bible. They are positive, decisive words. They require not only the agreement of your mind, but also confirmation in your heart and response in your actions.

Often non-Christians do not understand the true meaning of these words. They think that faith is a pie-in-the-sky kind of hope—something that may happen or may not. It is the same with belief. You will often hear people say, "You can believe anything, right or wrong, just as long as you believe something and it makes you feel better." This is not what the Bible teaches us about the faith, trust, and belief that we Christians have in our Heavenly Father, our Creator.

Faith (trust, belief) is our response to God, who loves us more than we can comprehend, who cares for us and is interested in every detail of our lives. Involved in this response is the fact that God actually confirms the truth about Jesus in the mind and heart of the Christian. Your faith means that you adhere to God, you commit each area of life to Him and rely upon the fact that your trust has been correctly placed in the one true God who will never leave you or forsake you.

Sometimes we are tempted to ask God to give us more faith. The problem is not that we need more faith, but it is that we need to use and exercise the faith we already have.

Study of the Bible and knowledge of what God's Word says are vital in building your faith. Faith must have an object and the object of your faith is God and the truth that He has revealed in His Word.

6

The Bible—God's Word

Second Timothy 3:16, 17 states, "The whole Bible was given to us by inspiration from God and is useful to teach us what is true and to make us realize what is wrong in our lives; it straightens us out and helps us do what is right. It is God's way of making us well prepared at every point, fully equipped to do good to everyone."

Do you remember that I told you in the beginning of this letter that the Bible is filled with promises and answers to every question and every need in our lives? I have quoted from *The Living Bible* because it is so easy to read, understand, and apply to your life. It is a

beautiful paraphrase of the Scriptures. I believe every
new Christian should have a copy with which to begin.
Later one of the new translations should be read in its
place. Linguistics has advanced so greatly in recent
years that many of the new editions are far more accurate and readable than the older ones.

Daily Bible reading is essential for all
Christians—old and new—for many reasons. Without
it, there will never be growth and maturity in our faith.
Our faith grows as we get to know more about Jesus. He
is not only our Savior, but our Friend and the Lord of
our lives. God created the world and each of us for His
glory. The whole Bible is "His Story." God's Word and
the learning of different verses that have special meaning to us are our best weapons against discouragement,
trials, and temptation. Read Psalms 119:11.

The first time I read the Bible, I was surprised and
delighted to find that every chapter had things to say
about the practical matters of everyday life. There has
been tremendous progress through the centuries in var-
ious endeavors, but the human heart has never
changed. We think, we act, and we reason the very
same way that mankind has since Creation. Without the
control of the Holy Spirit, people are naturally selfish
and self-centered, seeking those pleasures and com-
forts that will satisfy self.

Through our Bible reading, we learn why the Christian life is different from the way the non-Christian or natural person lives. We cannot live a life of joy and love in our own power. But God has the power to make it a reality in our lives, because the Holy Spirit indwells us and His Word tells us everything we need to know about Him. It is our guide to life, as His children. The key to success in the Christian life is being obedient to His Word. One reason why the Christian life is so exciting is because God continually reveals new truths to us in the Bible. Jesus said, "I am the Way, the Truth, and the Life."

The Bible says that the Word is food to the Christian. We all know how essential a balanced diet is to us physically. In the same way, we feed our souls with portions of the Word of God every day. Food is tastier when properly prepared; our Bible reading will be more meaningful when our hearts and minds are prepared, by asking God to give us understanding and wisdom as He guides us through the passages each day.

Read expectantly, underlining special verses as you go along. Try to read a shorter book in one sitting, so that you can grasp its continuity in the entirety. A book like *Unger's Bible Handbook* is nice to have as a reference because it gives a short history of each book in the Bible. It also gives a brief account of the content and the author.

I would like to suggest that every new Christian begin by reading the Gospel of John. It is the fourth book of the New Testament and gives an intimate glimpse of our personal Savior. After reading John, you will enjoy some of the shorter letters (Epistles) in the New Testament like: Colossians, Philippians, 1 John, and so forth. The Book of Acts is the history of the new Christian church. Many of these Epistles were written to the new churches mentioned in the Book of Acts.

Read with variety by reading two or three short books between the longer ones. Read all of the New Testament and save the Book of Revelation until the last. Before you delve into the Old Testament, whet your appetite by reading the Psalms and Proverbs. Then begin the books of Moses and the prophets.

For added study of God's Word, it is wonderful to attend a good Bible study with Christian friends. We need to have the fellowship and instruction of other Christians.

7

Choosing the Right Church

It is essential for believers to gather together for worship on the Lord's Day. The church where you worship and attend Sunday school will have a tremendous effect on your spiritual growth. Sometimes we are tempted to choose a church the way we would choose a book—by its title or cover. However, it is the content that has the real value. It is not always important to have a lovely building or belong to a certain denomination. Our decision should be based on the fact that in this church the Bible is preached, Jesus is honored, and the whole family can join together in the worship of God and the fellowship of believers.

In the book *The Family That Makes It,* published by Victor Books, there is an excellent chapter on selecting a church. I suggest that you read the book as soon as possible. And I urge you, dear friend, to wisely and carefully select a church where you sense the presence of our Lord and feel the warmth that comes from others who love Jesus as you do.

8

A Word About Our Home in Heaven

My letter to you has been lengthy, but I will soon be closing with many thoughts left unsaid. I have tried to help you begin this wonderful walk through life with Jesus and have intentionally saved the best part until the end. Yes, the best part for the Christian comes at the end of this earthly sojourn. God has promised us eternal life when we put our faith and trust in Jesus Christ as our Savior and Lord. Your eternal life begins when Jesus Christ comes into your life, and then never stops.

The Bible assures us that, when we leave our earthly life, we go directly to be with Jesus in heaven. The Bible talks of heaven as a magnificently glorious place. Beautiful beyond comprehension, but more wonderful than that—God is there and there is no suffering, pain, or death. Believers from every century, together praising God and filled with the love of Jesus. And to think we will spend eternity there. Because Jesus is alive today, you and I can have the assurance that we will live with Him also.

As I close, I want to share with you the words of one of my favorite hymns, "He Lives," which was written by Alfred H. Ackley.

I serve a risen Savior, He's in the world today;
I know that He is living, whatever men may
        say;
I see His hand of mercy, I hear His voice of
        cheer;
And just the time I need Him He's always
        near.

In all the world around me I see His loving
        care,
And tho my heart grows weary, I never will
        despair;

I know that He is leading thru all the stormy
blast.
The day of His appearing will come at last.

Rejoice, Rejoice, O Christian, lift up your
voice and sing
Eternal hallelujahs to Jesus Christ the King!
The hope of all who seek Him, the help of all
who find.
None other is so loving, so good and kind.

He lives, He Lives, Christ Jesus lives today!
He walks with me and talks with me along
life's narrow way.
He lives, He lives, salvation to impart!
You ask me how I know He lives?
He lives within my heart.

Is He living in your heart? I pray that now you
know for certain that you belong to Jesus. If there is
someone reading this letter who has never opened the
door of his heart to our Lord Jesus, I pray you will do it
now. There will never be a better time to place your
trust and faith in Jesus. May I share with you the two

verses that God used to bring me to Himself? "Now God says he will accept and acquit us—declare us 'not guilty'—if we trust Jesus Christ to take away our sins. And we all can be saved in this same way, by coming to Christ, no matter who we are or what we have been like" (Romans 3:22). The other verse is from Romans 12:2, "Don't copy the behavior and customs of this world, but be a new and different person with a fresh newness in all you do and think. Then you will learn from your own experience how his ways will really satisfy you." The more that I trust Him the more He has satisfied my every need. Won't you trust Him with your life today? All you have to do is come to Him in believing faith, praying: "Dear Jesus, I know that I am a sinner who needs You as my Savior. Please come into my life, forgive my sin, and make me the kind of person You want me to be. Thank You for loving me and for Your promise to give me a life that is 'totally new.' Amen."

"May the Lord bless and protect you; may the Lord's face radiate with joy because of you; may he be gracious to you, show you his favor, and give you his peace."

Numbers 6:24-26

Appendix 1

Getting Started

Beginning Bible Helps For:

Assurance
John 3:36
John 5:24
John 10:27-29
Romans 8:16
1 John 5:1, 10, 13; 3:14

Righting Wrong Prayer Life
Matthew 6:7, 8
John 3:14
Romans 8:26, 27
James 4:3; 5:16-18

Weaknesses in Life
John 8:31
Romans 12
Ephesians 4:29-32

Bible Study
John 5:39
Acts 17:11
Colossians 3:6
2 Timothy 2:15
1 Peter 2:2

Stewardship
Malachi 3:8-10
Matthew 6:33; 23:23
1 Corinthians 16:2
2 Corinthians 8:7

Spiritual Growth
1 Thessalonians 3:12
Hebrews 6:1
2 Peter 1:5; 3:18

What to Read When:

In Sorrow	John 14
In Danger	Psalms 91
God Seems Distant	Psalms 139
Discouraged	Isaiah 40
Faith Fails	Hebrews 11
You Are Blue	Psalms 34
Need Companionship	Psalms 23
You Are Worried	Matthew 6:19-34
You Need Forgiveness	Psalms 51
Life Seems Empty	John 15
You Feel Cheated	Psalms 103
Friends Fail You	Psalms 27
Sleepless	Psalms 4:4-8
You Are Angry	Matthew 5:9-22

Appendix 2

Evidences of Salvation

Love for Brethren	1 John 3:16
Witness of the Spirit	Romans 8:16
Guidance of the Spirit	Romans 8:14
Love of God Shed in Heart	Romans 5:5
Fruits of Spirit in Life	Galatians 5:22, 23
Keeping Christ's Commandments	1 John 2:3-6
Doing Righteousness	1 John 3:10
Overcoming the World	1 John 5:4

Appendix 3

Where to Find These Bible Treasures

Ten Commandments	Exodus 20
Lord's Prayer	Matthew 6
Beatitudes	Matthew 5:1-12
Sermon on the Mount	Matthew 5, 6, 7
Golden Rule	Matthew 7:12
Great Commission	Matthew 28:19, 20
Prodigal Son	Luke 15
Good Samaritan	Luke 10

Find Jesus Christ in God's Word

What Did Jesus Say About Himself?

Jesus made many claims during His earthly ministry. Look up the following verses and in your own
words write the meaning to the claims Jesus made about
Himself.

Matthew 28:19, 20
Mark 14:61, 62
John 10:11
John 10:30-33
John 14:6
John 14:8, 9

What Did Others Say About Jesus?

Throughout the Bible many people had things to
say about Jesus. Look up the following verses and see
what a few of them said.

Samaritan Woman	John 4:25-29
Jewish Leaders	John 5:18
Martha	John 11:27
Thomas	John 20:25-28
Peter	Matthew 16:16

The Character of Jesus

What do the following verses tell you concerning the character of Jesus?
Luke 23:33, 34
Mark 1:40-42
John 13:1-5
Matthew 19:14
John 2:13-16

Jesus Is God in the Flesh

How did He come into the world? Read Matthew 1:18-25 and summarize the circumstances surrounding the birth of Jesus.

Jesus, Your Own Personal Savior

Jesus is not only *the* Savior, but He is your own personal Savior. In your own words, explain what you know about Jesus.
Who is He?
Why did He come?
What effect does He have on your life?
What changes do you want Jesus to help you make in your life?

List areas where your attitudes and actions could
   be improved.
What can you do to show the love of Jesus to your
   family and friends?

List the names of your family members and friends
with whom you wish to share your faith in Jesus. Begin
to pray for the right opportunity and God's guidance in
talking to them about their relationship to our Lord,
Jesus.

Appendix 5

How to Succeed in the Christian Life

Rely Upon the Holy Spirit. Ephesians 5:18; Acts 1:8

Confess Jesus as Lord. Romans 10:9, 10; Phillippians 2:11

Pray Without Ceasing. 1 Thessalonians 5:17; Luke 18:1

Search the Scriptures Daily. John 5:39; Acts 17:11

Attend Public Worship Regularly. Hebrews 10:25; Psalms 50:5

Give Liberally Without Grudging. 2 Corinthians 9:7; Luke 6:38

Give Attention to Missions. John 4:35; 36; Matthew 28:19, 20

Forget Self–Live for Others. Matthew 20:26-28; 1 John 3:16

Witness to Someone Daily. Acts 2:42, 46, 47

Carry Your Bible or Testament With You. Titus 1:9; Philippians 2:16

Appendix 6

Additional Helps

The verses of Scripture that I have quoted have been taken from *The Living Bible*. I wholeheartedly recommend this paraphrase of the Scripture for every new believer in Christ Jesus. It is easy to read, understand, and follow. God has used it in a mighty way to enlighten and deepen the Christian life of countless millions of people. I hope you will soon have your copy of *The Living Bible*.

"A word should be said here about paraphrases. What are they? To paraphrase is to say something in different words than the author used. It is a restatement of an author's thoughts, using different words than he did. This book is a paraphrase of the Old and New Testaments. Its purpose is to say as exactly as possible what the writers of the Scriptures meant, and to say it simply, expanding where necessary for a clear understanding by the modern reader" (from the preface to *The Living Bible*).

As your working knowledge of the Bible expands, you may wish to purchase one of the new and very accurate translations of the Bible. Your pastor or the owner of your local Christian bookstore can help you select one.

There are many excellent materials available for your personal study or for group study of the Bible. They are too numerous to mention here, but I would like to mention three that are presently available.

1. *Ten Basic Steps Toward Christian Maturity*, Campus Crusade for Christ, Inc., Arrowhead Springs, San Bernardino, California, 92414.
2. *Studies in Christian Living*, Navigators, Navpress, P.O. Box 1659, Colorado Springs, Colorado 80901.
3. *Life's New Beginnings*, Stonecroft Ministries, 10121 Grandview Road, Kansas City, Missouri 64137.

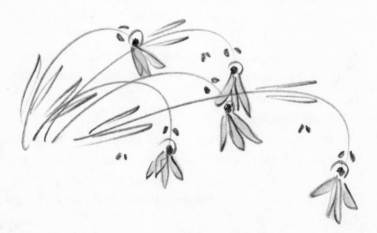